D0601856

REAL-LIFE
DRAGONS

EDGE
BOOKS

SEA DRAGONS

by Jody S. Rake

Consultant:
Dr. Adam Jones, Professor
Department of Biology
Texas A&M University
College Station, Texas

CAPSTONE PRESS
a capstone imprint

Edge Books are published by Capstone Press,
1710 Roe Crest Drive, North Mankato, Minnesota 56003
www.mycapstone.com

Library of Congress Cataloging-in-Publication Data
Cataloging-in-Publication Data is available from the Library of Congress Website.
ISBN 978-1-5157-5072-7 (library binding)
ISBN 978-1-5157-5076-5 (papreback)
ISBN 978-1-5157-5088-8 (eBook PDF)
Summary: Discusses the habitat, life cycle, and behavior of the sea dragon

Editorial Credits
Abby Colich, editor; Bobbie Nuytten, designer; Pam Mitsaoks, media researcher;
Steve Walker, production specialist

Image Credits
Alamy: Erik Schlogl, 28, WaterFrame, 23 middle right; Dreamstime: Zepherwind,
6; Getty Images: Orlando Sentinel, 14, Shin Okamoto, 12-13; Minden Pictures:
Alex Mustard/NPL, 20, John Lewis/Auscape, 22-23 bottom; Shutterstock:
archana bhartia, 26, Bernhard Richter, 24, Dmytro Pylypenko, 17, fenkieandreas,
9, Kjersti Joergensen, 4, MG photos, 7, Michael Warwick, cover right, Oliver
Koch, 10-11, Rich Carey, 27 top, Sebastien Burel, 8, Sergey Dubrov, 18, Studio
37, 15 bottom, Sura Nualpradid, 5; SuperStock/Norbert Wu, 25; Thinkstock:
LagunaticPhoto, 16, Whitepointer, 19

Design Elements:
Shutterstock: Andrii_M, Fantom666, Limbad, yyang

Printed and bound in the USA.
10028S17CG

TABLE OF CONTENTS

CHAPTER I

LIVING LEGENDS OF THE SEA

Off the coast of Australia, a forest of seaweed gently sways. A small leafy mass breaks away. As it drifts gracefully, it becomes clear this is not a plant. It is an animal. Its body is colorful and flashy. It has a pointy snout. In fact, it looks like a dragon! This creature is a kind of fish called a sea dragon.

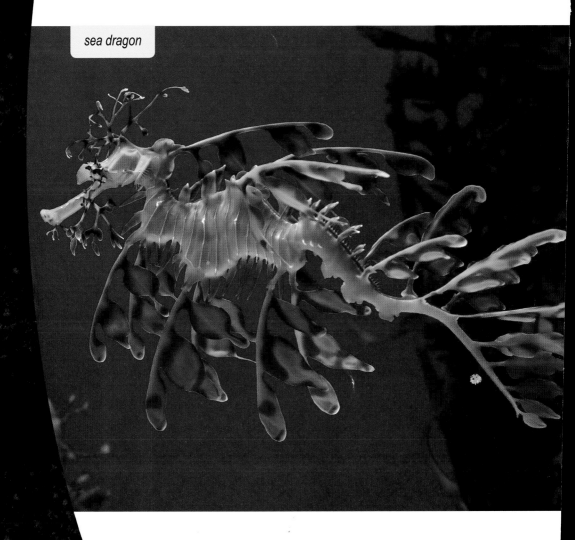

sea dragon

DRAGONS—MYTH AND REALITY

You've probably read about dragons in books. Dragons of fiction are often scaly and snakelike. Others, such as those of Chinese legends, are frilly and **ornate**. Sometimes real-life animals look like these **mythical** creatures. These animals have earned the name "dragon" for how they look or behave. The sea dragon is one such animal.

ornate—richly decorated
mythical—imaginary or possibly not real

THE THREE SEA DRAGONS

The ocean is home to three **species** of sea dragons. The leafy sea dragon is the most eye-catching. It is named for its many leaflike **appendages**. These frilly branches are not fins. They are not used for swimming. Instead they provide **camouflage**. The delicate frills gently sway like the surrounding seaweed.

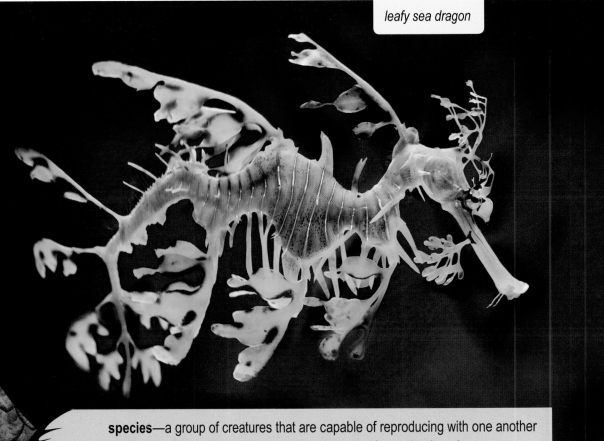

leafy sea dragon

species—a group of creatures that are capable of reproducing with one another
appendage—a limb or other part that sticks out of an animal or plant
camouflage—coloring or covering that makes animals, people, and objects look like their surroundings

The weedy sea dragon is also called the common sea dragon. It has fewer and smaller attachments than its leafy cousin. But its colorful markings make it equally beautiful.

Recently scientists discovered a third species of sea dragon. The ruby sea dragon is bright red. It is less common than the other two species. It lives in deeper waters than the leafies and weedies. Not much is known about this species.

SEA DRAGON SIZE

Sea dragons are much smaller than the dragons of stories. They range from about 14 to 18 inches (35 to 45 centimeters) long. Weedy sea dragons are typically the largest.

weedy sea dragon

FISHY DRAGONS

Sea dragons may not be what you imagine when you think of fish. But like other fish, sea dragons spend their entire lives in water. Their gills help them take in **oxygen**. Fins help them move. Their young hatch from eggs. These similarities led scientists to **classify** sea dragons as fish.

DRAGON FACT

One species of pipefish is called the dragon pipefish. It is not as fancy as the sea dragons, but it has a dragon-like head.

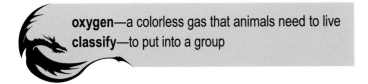

oxygen—a colorless gas that animals need to live
classify—to put into a group

pipefish

SEA DRAGON RELATIVES

Sea dragons are related to two other similar-looking fish—sea horses and pipefish. Sea dragons and their relatives don't have scales like other fish. Instead their bodies are covered with hard, bony plates. The bony plates look like rings around their bodies. The heads of sea dragons and their relatives resemble a horse's head. They have long, tubelike snouts. A tiny mouth at the tip sucks in food.

sea horse

CHAPTER 2

LIFE IN A LEAFY LOCALE

Leafy and weedy sea dragons live near the coasts of western and southern Australia. Here it is neither very cold nor very warm. The water temperature ranges from 55 degrees Fahrenheit (13 degrees Celsius) in the winter to 75°F (24°C) in the summer.

Leafy and weedy sea dragons live in shallow water. Their homes are rocky and sandy **reefs**, seaweed beds, and sea grass meadows. The seaweeds and sea grasses provide protection from **predators** and strong ocean **currents**. Both leafy and weedy sea dragons live no deeper than 82 feet (25 meters).

Scientists believe the ruby sea dragon lives in deeper and darker waters. Its red color looks gray to predators. This color camouflages it in the dark water.

reef—an underwater strip of rocks, coral, or sand near the surface of the ocean

predator—an animal that hunts another animal for food

current—the movement of water in a river or ocean

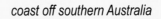
coast off southern Australia

DRAGON FACT

In Australia the current season is
the opposite of what it is in North America
or Europe. The Australian winter is mid-June
through mid-September. Summer runs December
through March.

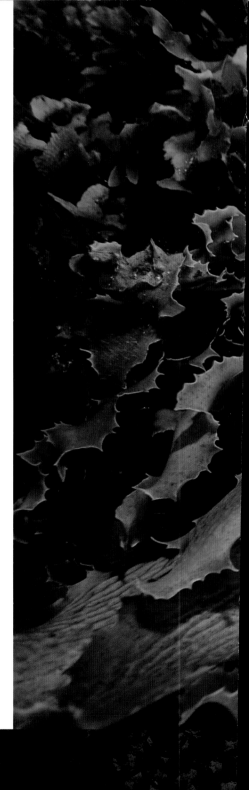

HIDDEN IN PLAIN SIGHT

Possible predators lurk in all directions. Sea dragons must rely on some form of protection. For this creature it's all about camouflage. Sea dragons have some of the best camouflage on Earth.

The sea dragons' home is one of swaying seaweeds. Sunlight peeks through from above. When a leafy sea dragon sticks close to a seaweed bed, it is almost impossible for would-be predators to see. Its frills blend in with the seaweed.

The weedy sea dragon looks very different from its leafy relative. It is less frilly. Its leaflike appendages are smaller. Its body is reddish-brown. The dull reddish-brown is marked with bright yellow and purple spots and stripes. Scientists aren't sure why it looks the way it does. Its colors could help it attract mates. It could be to show **dominance**. Its colors could also help it hide in the dappled light of the sea grass meadows.

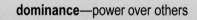

dominance—power over others

This leafy sea dragon blends in with ocean plants.

DRAGON FACT

The leafy sea dragon can also change colors! At times its drab green changes to soft purples.

CHAPTER 3

SEA DRAGONS ON THE MOVE

Sea dragons don't look like other fish. They don't move like them either. Sea dragons are not strong or fast swimmers. Their bony bodies don't move easily. They lack the **streamlined** body shape of most fish. Also, sea dragons lack tail fins, which other fish species use to propel them in the water.

A sea dragon usually flows slowly with the currents. The slow movements trick predators into thinking the sea dragon is a drifting plant. Tiny, transparent fins help a sea dragon along. A **dorsal fin** on its back moves it forward. **Pectoral fins** on either side of its neck help it steer. The fins rapidly vibrate. It uses its tail to help it turn.

A swim bladder inside the sea dragon keeps it from sinking. It lets the sea dragon stay at the same depth without wasting energy on swimming. The swim bladder is full of air. The fish can increase or decrease the amount of air. It moves up or down in the water depending on how much air is inside.

pectoral fin

dorsal fin

Tails

Sea horses have **prehensile** tails. The tails can curl and grip seaweed stalks. Sea dragons, on the other hand, have tails that are not prehensile. They cannot grab onto anything with their tails.

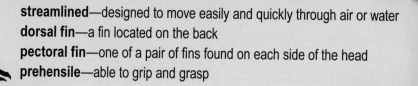

streamlined—designed to move easily and quickly through air or water
dorsal fin—a fin located on the back
pectoral fin—one of a pair of fins found on each side of the head
prehensile—able to grip and grasp

CHAPTER 4

DINING SEA DRAGON STYLE

If you spot a sea dragon in the ocean, there's one thing it's probably doing—eating! A sea dragon must eat all the time in order to survive. It has no stomach. Food passes through its body very quickly. A sea dragon also doesn't have any teeth. At the end of its thin snout is a tiny mouth. The snout works like a straw. It sucks in food from the sea.

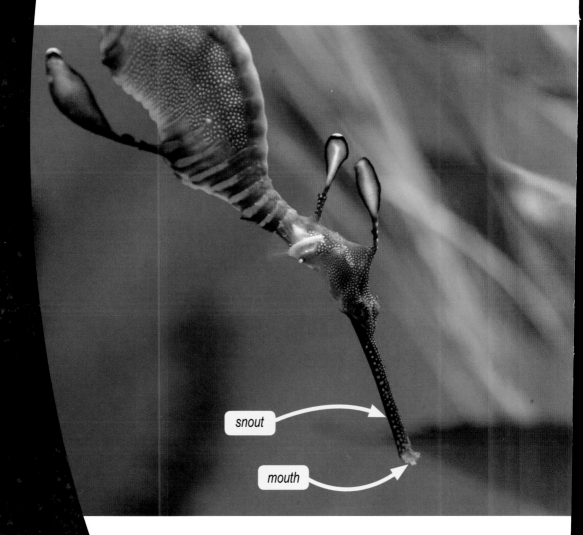

snout

mouth

A sea dragon eats **plankton**. Plankton is composed of tiny shrimp, fish **larvae**, and other very small **prey**. These tiny animals drift through the sea. Plankton are everywhere in the ocean. Sea dragons don't have to hunt for their food. They are usually surrounded by it. As plankton floats by, sea dragons suck it in and swallow it whole.

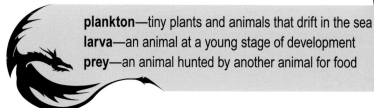

plankton—tiny plants and animals that drift in the sea
larva—an animal at a young stage of development
prey—an animal hunted by another animal for food

krill, a shrimplike type of plankton

DRAGON FACT

Every 24 hours a sea dragon may gulp down thousands of plankton!

STAYING SAFE IN A WORLD OF HUNTERS

Sea dragons live in a sea full of predators. They share space with giant 8-foot (2.4-m) long groupers. Even great white sharks lurk nearby! Yet sea dragons themselves are almost never preyed upon. How do they manage to stay off the menu?

Their camouflage keeps them well protected. The size and shape of their bodies is another factor. To large, hungry hunters, sea dragons are just tiny morsels of food. Their bony bodies offer little nourishment. Sea dragons just aren't worth the effort to large predators.

grouper

Leafy sea dragons have some extra protection. Long spines run down their backs and sides. Most ocean predators avoid spiny animals.

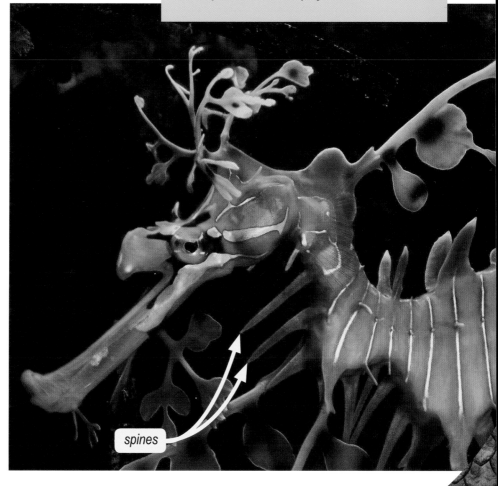

spines

CHAPTER 5

SEA DRAGON LIFE CYCLE

Sea dragons come together to mate once a year. The female lays 75 to 300 tiny eggs on the male. The eggs look like little, round balls. The male **incubates** them. He carries them for six to eight weeks.

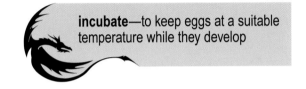

incubate—to keep eggs at a suitable temperature while they develop

eggs

When the eggs start to hatch, the male releases a few at a time. It takes a few hours to a few days to release all the eggs. The babies, called fry, hatch tail first. They have short snouts and lack the leafy appendages of the adults.

From the moment they hatch, sea dragons are on their own. They settle to the seafloor. Then they eat the still-attached egg sac. In about two days, their snouts are bigger. They start feeding on plankton.

Sea Dragon Dads

Male sea dragons, sea horses, and pipefish have special body parts for incubating eggs. Male sea horses and pipefish have a pouch on the belly. The male sea dragon has no pouch. Instead, he holds the eggs on a patch under his tail. The flesh on the patch is spongy and soft. When the eggs are laid, it hardens. It forms a protective cup around each egg.

GROWING UP SEA DRAGON

Eating around the clock, sea dragons grow steadily until they are about two years old. Then they are adults. They may keep growing, but more slowly.

No one knows for sure how long sea dragons live in the wild. Scientists believe weedy sea dragons live five to seven years. Leafies may live about seven to 10 years. In an aquarium they can both live up to 10 years.

leafy sea dragon, about one week old

HANGING OUT DRAGON STYLE

Sea dragons are solitary animals. They usually hang out alone. Sometimes they hang out in pairs. In the early spring, they gather in groups. By early summer they will find their mates.

pair of weedy sea dragons

CHAPTER 6
SEA DRAGONS IN DANGER

Sea dragons face many threats. Ocean pollution is one of the biggest threats. Toxic chemicals and fertilizer run off from the land into the ocean. They can poison these delicate fishes and their prey.

Pollution in the ocean can affect all sea life.

Sea dragons can also be the victims of their own beauty. They are often chased and harassed by divers. The stress can cause them not to eat or reproduce. Sea dragons are also much sought after for home aquariums. Poachers illegally catch them in the wild and sell them in the pet trade.

DRAGON FACT

Sea dragons cannot withstand strong winter storms. Their bodies are often found washed up on beac

diver with a leafy sea dragon

PROTECTING AN UNCOMMON SPECIES

Because they only live in one area of the world, sea dragons are not as common as some other fish. Very little is known about them. Scientists don't know how many are in the wild. Because of this, sea dragons receive special protection. Australia has laws in place to protect sea dragons.

The International Union for the Conservation of Nature (IUCN) first classified sea dragons in 2006. The IUCN is one of the world's largest groups devoted to protecting all animals. It classifies sea dragons as Near Threatened. This means the animal is not yet threatened or endangered, but could be soon. This will help protect them while scientists study them more.

Ocean currents carry litter thousands of miles.

You Can Help Too

Even if you live thousands of miles from sea dragons, you can still help them. Only certain public aquariums are allowed to house sea dragons. If you see one at a pet store, don't buy it! Tell your parents or an adult to notify the IUCN. Protect their homes by taking care of the ocean. Don't litter at the beach—or anywhere. Ocean litter can travel thousands of miles. Small acts can add up to a big difference!

SEA DRAGON FACTS

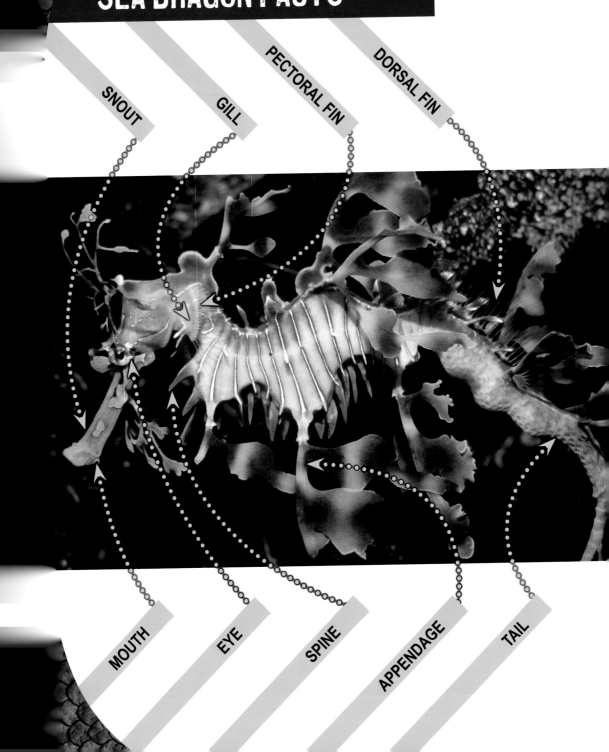

SNOUT

GILL

PECTORAL FIN

DORSAL FIN

MOUTH

EYE

SPINE

APPENDAGE

TAIL

SPECIES:
leafy, weedy, and ruby

RANGE:
coasts off western and southern Australia

HABITAT:
coastal seaweed and sea grass beds

SIZE:
about 14 to 18 inches (35 to 45 cm) long

PREY:
plankton, tiny shrimp, and fish larvae

PREDATORS:
rarely any, sometimes large fish

LIFE SPAN:
about five to 10 years in the wild; about 10 years in captivity

GLOSSARY

appendage (uh-PEN-dij)—a limb or other part that sticks out of an animal or plant

camouflage (KA-muh-flahzh)—coloring or covering that makes animals, people, and objects look like their surroundings

classify (KLAS-uh-fy)—to put into a group

current (KUHR-uhnt)—the movement of water in a river or ocean

dominance (DAH-muhn-uhns)—power over others

dorsal fin (DOR-suhl FIN)—a fin located on the back

incubate (INK-yoo-bate)—to keep eggs at a suitable temperature while they develop

larva (LAR-vuh)—an animal at a young stage of development

mythical (MITH-i-kuhl)—imaginary or possibly not real

ornate (or-NAYT)—richly decorated

oxygen (OK-suh-juhn)—a colorless gas that animals need to live

pectoral fin (PECKT-or-uhl FIN)—one of a pair of fins found on each side of the head

plankton (PLANGK-tuhn)—tiny plants and animals that drift in the sea

predator (PRED-uh-tur)—an animal that hunts another animal for food

prehensile (pree-HENSS-ile)—able to grip and grasp

prey (PRAY)—an animal hunted by another animal for food

reef (REEF)—an underwater strip of rocks, coral, or sand near the surface of the ocean

species (SPEE-sheez)—a group of creatures that are capable of reproducing with one another

streamlined (STREEM-lined)—designed to move easily and quickly through air or water

READ MORE

Leaf, Christina. *Sea Horses*. Ocean Life Up Close. Minneapolis: Bellwether Media, 2017.

Meister, Cari. *Sea Dragons*. Life Under the Sea. Minneapolis: Bullfrog Books, 2015.

Peterson, Megan Cooley. *Coral Reefs*. Smithsonian Little Explorer. North Mankato, Minn.: Capstone Press, 2014.

INTERNET SITES

FactHound offers a safe, fun way to find Internet sites related to this book. All of the sites on FactHound have been researched by our staff.

Here's all you do:

Visit *www.facthound.com*

Type in this code: 9781515750727

Check out projects, games and lots more at
www.capstonekids.com

CRITICAL THINKING USING THE COMMON CORE

1. Where do sea dragons live? Name two characteristics of this place. (Key Idea and Details)

2. Look at the photos on pages 6 and 7. How are the two sea dragons alike? How are they different? (Integration of Knowledge and Ideas)

3. Reread pages 20 and 21. Use the callout box to define the word *incubate*. Then explain how a male sea dragon incubates eggs. (Craft and Structure)

INDEX